MOSHI MOSHI MUSUBI

Say *Hello-Hello* to the Spam Sandwich
A Sushi Snack and Appetizer Treat

Mainland Twists to the Hawaiian Island Favorite

Debra D. Hayashi

This book is for all the Foodies who celebrate the unique flavors and combinations that the world of cuisine has to offer and who embrace the adventure to explore their own creativity by experimenting in the kitchen to educate and delight their pallet and then share their discoveries with family and friends.

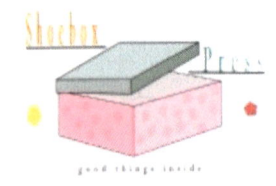

©2015 by Debra D. Hayashi and Published by Shoebox Press
All Rights Reserved. No part of this publication may be reproduced in any form or by any means including scanning, photocopying, or otherwise without prior written permission by the copyright holder

TABLE OF CONTENT

I. INTRODUCTION

II. CLASSIC MUSUBI RECIPES

CLASSIC TERIYAKI MUSUBI

Tutorials & Inspiration:

The Hands On of Hand Made:

- ➢ CLASSIC MUSUBI RECIPE #2
- ➢ CLASSIC MUSUBI RECIPE #3

III. MY MAINLAND MUSUBI MADNESS – Musubi with a Twist!

- ➢ Recipe #1 - MUSUBI CALIFORNIA ROLL
- ➢ Recipe #2 - MUSUBI TACO
- ➢ Recipe #3 - MUSUBI MAC & CHEESE
- ➢ Recipe #4 - BREAKFAST MUSUBI #1
- ➢ Recipe #5 - BREAKFAST MUSUBI #2
- ➢ Recipe #6 - BBQ MUSUBI
- ➢ Recipe #7 - OCTOBER FEST MUSUBI
- ➢ Recipe #8 - TEX-MEX CHILI MUSUBI
- ➢ Recipe #9 - FRUITY MUSUBI
- ➢ Recipe #10 - SPAM & CHEESE MUSUBI

- Recipe #11 – FRENCH DIP MUSUBI
- Recipe #12 - CHICKEN FRIED STEAK MUSUBI
- Recipe #13 – MUSUBI PIZZA
- Recipe #14 – PB&J MUSUBI
- Recipe #15 – CUCUMBER & HUMUS MUSUBI
- Recipe #16 – BLT MUSUBI
- Recipe #17 – VEGGIE MUSUBI
- Recipe #18 – MUSUBI LEFTOVERS
- Recipe #19 – STIR-FRY MUSUBI
- Recipe #20 – YOUR OWN MUSUBI CREATION

IV. APPETIZERS & TINY TASTE TREATS

- MUSUBI RICE BALLS
- MUSUBI CANAPES

V. GLOSSARY OF INGREDIENTS

VI. MUSUBI MAKING PARTY

- **OCCASIONS TO SERVE MUSUBIS**

VII. FINAL THOUGHTS

I.   INTRODUCTION

Have you ever heard of Musubi? Sounds like it could be the latest dance craze, or perhaps a new exercise program, right? It means "knot" or "to put two things together." Pronounced either, Moo-soo-bee (without any inflection), or Moo-SOO-BEE, either way is correct; however my friend, a Hawaiian Island Native, insists it is the former so I have adopted it as my preferred pronunciation. And if you have ever lived in, or visited Hawaii, you already know that a Musubi is a favorite island sandwich or snack made with Nori (Japanese Seaweed in paper thin sheets), Steamed Sushi Rice, and Grilled SPAM (Spiced Canned Ham.) Put them altogether and you get SPAM MUSUBI, also known as "the poor-man's sushi," or a SPAM sandwich.

SPAM is a popular staple of any Hawaiian pantry and it was introduced to the Islands during WWII when it was part of the GI K-rations. It was adopted by the locals and is added to many Hawaiian dishes from breakfast to dinner and most meals in between. Musubi is popular as a sandwich in bento boxes or as a snack item, and while easy to make at home, it is also found in mini-markets and 7-Elevens at the check-out register. It is available at fast-food chains and it is even included on upscale restaurant menus.

SPAM may sound unappetizing to some, but don't let that stop you from trying this wonderful sandwich or appetizer. SPAM now comes in many flavors, and as you will see in this book, the right sauce can make even the most skeptical among you perk up your taste buds and say, "Oishii!" (Delicious/Tastes Good)

The Back Story - Evolution of an Idea:

My husband, Michael, and I were personally introduced to this fabulous tasty treat through his family, when a cousin, at a family outing, happened to make them as sandwich snacks packed into lunches given to all the golfers to take along in our golf carts. We never knew such a simple delight existed. And to learn that it was made with grilled SPAM was even more intriguing. Although I remember trying SPAM as a kid, it wasn't something my mother often kept in the pantry, and Michael and I had never kept SPAM in our own home, so we were quite surprised by how much we liked it this way. As lovers of food – both eating and creating it - we naturally were anxious to learn how to make Musubis for ourselves.

We quickly discovered that there is very little needed in the way of tools or ingredients. Most important is a Gata – a little silicon or acrylic musubi mold, but even this is optional, it just makes it easier to assemble and the Musubis come out very neat and uniformed. This, along with a few simple ingredients is all that is necessary to create this uniquely satisfying snack. Fast forward a number of years…

This past Thanksgiving, in California, my hubby and I stopped by a local Asian Market to pick up senbei rice crackers, when he noticed the Musubi molds on display and decided to pick one up to give to his sister whose family was hosting our visit as well as the family's Thanksgiving Feast. We then selected the ingredients needed to make a classic musubi: Nori (wafer thin sheets of seaweed) and Furikake (rice seasonings - which come in numerous varieties available in Asian markets and Ethnic food sections at some local grocers), and a can of SPAM. These would be added to the steamed rice. We anticipated how these would be layered into the musubi mold, pressed and rolled into "bricks," then cut sushi roll style, and served as a delicious appetizer. Naturally, the extended family gathering practically inhaled them with great enthusiasm; the platter disappeared in a matter of minutes, with little ones shoving the whole piece at once into their mouths, making them look like athletes with funny mouth guards, as the rest of us laughingly hoped they wouldn't choke on them.

It then occurred to me that these wonderfully simple rolls could be made with just about any ingredient one might desire, or that one could stomach. Couldn't they? Just like "real" sushi rolls. And it also occurred to me that these little gems were not widely known, even in their purest form. I am exceedingly surprised that musubi has yet to become as well known here on the mainland as say such better known fare as: sushi, egg rolls, pizza, burgers, tacos, burritos, wraps, etc., as a popular luncheon choice that can be tweaked in a limitless variety of combinations. Especially with the number of people who vacation in Hawaii every year, and who, no doubt, have discovered and tried a musubi at least once as part of their initiation into island life.

This brings me to the reason for this cookbook and collection of recipes. First, as I have just stated, I think Musubi is a sorely overlooked cuisine here in the continental United States and I would like to raise awareness by introducing (or re introducing) this unique treat to the mainstream mainland population. Second, I would like to expose the audience to my creative combinations. Lastly, I hope to inspire others to create their own favorite Musubi recipes. For though I love the simplicity and flavor of the classic Musubi, I believe the possibilities are endless, only limited to ones imagination for the selection of ingredients and one's own pallet preferences to create the ultimate variety of Modern Musubi "classics."

We are all familiar with the classic pizza, classic taco, classic burger and hot dog, or even the classic California roll. Most of us have seen those shows on the Food Channel featuring food trucks and diners where chefs are crafting their specialty tacos, burgers and fabulous gourmet meals out of a simple sandwich. Each of these has been tweaked and re-invented into countless variations with the seemingly limitless choices of cheeses, meats, veggies, fruits, sauces, infused flavors, and toppings that are used in the creation of fantastic food fare.

We savor our choices, from New York to Chicago Style, from Tex-Mex to Southwest BBQ, or Southern-Fried; be it spicy to tangy, or sweet and sour. From Meat lovers to Vegetarians, we Americans love to switch it up and mix it up just to shake things up while constructing flavorful, if perhaps strange, but delicious groupings within every food genre. And nowhere is this desire for diversity more prevalent than with our sandwich, appetizer, and snacking foods. A banana, mayonnaise, peanut butter on white bread sandwich comes to mind. And with this in mind, the next logical thought was that there should be a cookbook, or a collection of recipes that would put a mainland twist to these wonderful sandwiches so the masses could know and enjoy this Hawaiian classic snack food and discover the musubi. And if I am successful I will hopefully inspire others to experiment and have fun making their own unique combos and to begin packing them in lunches or presenting their creations to friends and family at their next potluck, tailgater, book club, bunco game, or holiday party. And then perhaps a new "Musubi Craze" will take off with everyone wondering where the Musubi has been all their life. Move aside pigs-in-a-blanket and tortilla roll-ups. Look out meatballs and potato skins. **It's time to make Musubis!**

II. CLASSIC MUSUBI RECIPES

This is one of the easiest and most traditional types of Musubi sandwich, and the basic techniques described below will be used in making any other kind of musubi. The only variation will be in the order of layering and the selection of ingredients used in each of the recipes.

CLASSIC TERIYAKI MUSUBI

Makes 4 Large Musubi Bricks/Logs - sliced into 24 pieces.

INGREDIENTS -

* 4 Sheets of Nori

* 4 Cups Steamed Rice (Use medium grain sushi rice cooked in a rice cooker or stovetop following package instructions). You can also make sweet sushi rice by adding Mirin which is a Japanese rice wine available in Asian markets and some Ethnic Food sections at local markets.

* SPAM - marinated and then grilled in a teriyaki sauce (purchased or per recipe below)

* Furikake Flakes (optional) - a rice condiment of seaweed and sesame seeds, but many varieties are available.

* Musubi Mold Maker - (most useful, inexpensive to purchase at Asian Markets or online, but could use a small size SPAM can as a mold by cutting out the bottom, or just form the mususbi free-hand – use plastic wrap to roll).

* A small bowl of water.

* Serrated knife

PREPARATION:

Rice -

* Wash 4 cups of white, medium sushi rice and put in rice cooker with 4 cups of water - set to cook. If you don't have a rice cooker, prepare on stovetop per package directions.

Marinade -

* While the rice is cooking you can prepare the Teriyaki marinade. In a 10 or 12 inch frying pan, combine equal parts of the following ingredients: For this recipe I am using 1/2 cup for each Part, but you can use ¼ to 1 cup portions depending on the number of Musubis you want to make.

1 Part Granulated Sugar

1 Part Soy Sauce (Regular or Low Sodium)

1 Part Mirin -Japanese Sweet Rice Wine available in the ethnic section of most supermarkets

1 clove Garlic and some grated Ginger are optional additions.

Stir over low-medium heat until sugar is dissolved. Set aside to cool. Once cooled to room temperature, add the slices of SPAM to marinade.

SPAM -

Remove SPAM from its can and slice in half, then slice each half into 4 equal slices, approximately 1/4 inch in thickness. (Some people even use an egg slicer to begin or to evenly mark the cuts). Place these into the Teriyaki sauce, allowing them to marinade for 15-30 minutes. Then place the marinated SPAM slices into the frying pan and grill on each side. Lastly, add some of the teriyaki sauce and continue to sauté SPAM slices. Turn off heat.

If you don't want to marinade the spam you can just add it to the fry pan to sauté a bit longer after slices have grilled.

Note: You could also just buy a bottle of your favorite Teriyaki Sauce in a bottle and use instead of starting from scratch.

ASSEMBLE:

* If using the long size Gata/Musubi mold, you will use one full sheet of Nori per Musubi roll you create. If using the smaller mold you will want to cut Nori Sheets in half to create four equal sheets.
* Lay the sheet of Nori on your work surface. Place the musubi mold lengthwise on top of the nori sheet about 1/2 to 2/3rds down the on the sheet.
* Wet the spoon by dipping into the dish of water and shaking off the excess. Scoop out a couple of spoonful's of cooked rice to fill musubi mold with a thin layer. Lightly press rice down with the spoon to gently cover the nori about 1/4 inch thick.
* Next sprinkle a light layer of your favorite Furikake flakes over the rice.
* Add a layer of grilled SPAM - one for a small mold; lay two slices across end-to-end for a large mold.
* Then sprinkle another layer of Furikake flakes.
* Lastly top the whole thing with another layer of rice.
* Now take the lid or top of your Musubi maker. Dip your fingers into the water dish and swipe over the bottom of the press to moisten slightly and prevent it from sticking to the rice. Now place it in the mold and press down to firmly pack all the layers together.
* Remove the mold and set aside. *Tip:* Continue to hold the press down on the musubi to keep it in place as you grasp ahold of the sides of the mold and pull up.
* Lift one side of the nori sheet and wrap around all the layers. Wetting your fingers again, apply a little water along the remaining edge and wrap it around to meet up with the other end and seal the sheet together. The water helps to make a nice seal.

You now have a Musubi BRICK.

Set aside for a few moments while you begin all over again, repeating each step to make a second, third and fourth Musubi brick.

Once you have completed assembling all your Musubi bricks, you take up your serrated knife, wetting the blade and gently wiping off the excess water - this will help prevent the knife from sticking to the bricks as you slice it into equal portions. Repeat the wetting and drying off the knife between each slice.

To slice - first slice your Musubi block in half. Then slice each half into 3 equal slices to make a total of 6 sushi roll sized pieces. Or they can be cut into triangular shapes. Place these on a platter and serve as is, or add a bowl of dipping sauce such as soy sauce with wasabi, sweet chili sauce or Sriracha mixed with mayonnaise and a side of fresh ginger. That's all there is to it. It may sound a bit laborious at first, but it really is quite quick and easy once you get going and it's a lot of fun to do. If you've ever played with playdough and molds, you can assemble a Musubi. The results of your effort will be extremely satisfying.

Tutorials & Inspiration:

If you feel unsure about the assembly process, it turns out there are any number of videos available on YouTube demonstrating the whole process, sharing plenty of techniques to give you all the confidence you need to proceed. And as I refer you to YouTube and Pinterest for more tips and examples of Musubi creativity, you will see that even though I quite organically discovered my initial thought that Musubis could be more than the traditional classic, it obviously is not such a new idea after all. Others have already come to the same conclusion and are attempting to develop and share their recipes. But the fact that Musubi is not widely known and enjoyed is still true.

When I first suggested to family members that I thought musubi was perfect for creative tweaking, some scoffed at the thought of improving on a classic, others were willing to consider the possibility. And if you are reading this I'm sure you are curious as well. Even though others were already sharing their creations, the fact remains there is little mainstream knowledge of the musubi. It isn't exactly "trending" out there. I couldn't find a simple cookbook to inspire and spread the word. So I am thankful for these creative chefs and their tutorials that I can suggest to you as part of my goal to make Musubi, and Musubi Making, Mainstream! I hold to my original premise that the world at large needs to become more aware of its existence.
My mission is to make Musubi Madness come alive for the masses.

With that all said, I would like to give a shout-out to a couple of Pinterest links with great tutorials and blogs; and also three shout-outs to some creative cooks and their YouTube channels that I think you should enjoy.

If you go to Pinterest you can search the word Musubi and come up with many, many great pins for recipes and tips on making Musubi.

>One I would suggest you visit is an excellent blog: *Sandra's Alaska Recipes* http://sandrarecipeblogsite.blogspot.com/2010/08/hawaiian-spam-musubi.html
>
>She provides a simple but terrific recipe for *Hawaiian Spam Musubi* that includes detailed photos of each step of preparation.
>
>The second Pinterest pin I would like to recommend is one that takes you to another terrific blog, *Cook and Be Merry* by Lynne Hemmer: http://cookandbemerry.com/hawaiian-spam-musubi/ where she gives a wonderful history of SPAM, how it became a staple of Hawaii and the origin of musubi. She also shares her recipes and ideas for beautiful musubi presentation.

You can do the same on YouTube. Type in Musubi and you again will find a great many tutorial videos on how to make musubi.

>But the first YouTube channel I'd like you to visit is *Honeysuckle* and her *HoneysuckleCatering Channel*. She is proof that people love to put their own spin on classic foods and traditional recipes. It is human nature, and she shows a great way to make her own recipe of Pineapple Glaze Musubi, so go to:

> https://www.youtube.com/watch?v=cNSynV3q3Aw
>
> She also gives a quick demonstration on how to make a simple musubi without a mold, plus she grills her SPAM on the BBQ rather than pan frying and grilling, which shows this is a great idea for tailgating and family BBQs. You can find her at https://www.youtube.com/watch?v=DjlY6IP-kio

Next you should go to another channel I discovered that some of you foodies may already know. Check out: *"You CAN Musubi with Lanai and Chef Adam"*
https://www.youtube.com/watch?v=xqW2oT818E0

> They are from Aloha Plate and are the winners of The Great Food Truck Race, Season Four. They also suggest you check out http://www.spam.com for their great videos and recipes. They will give you quick and delicious inspiration for some ideas I had myself, again before I even heard of creating unusual Musubi recipes.
>
> And last, but not least, check out Richard Blaine's channel as he has some "gourmet" musubi recipes I'm sure you'll enjoy. His channel can be found at https://www.youtube.com/watch?v=WfCQvjAbxWY

These are just a few to review and I know you will see from their examples that Musubi making can be fun and creative and a delicious change from your usual sandwich and appetizer repertoire.

The Hands On of Hand Made:

What follows next are a few more Classic Recipe combinations. I will list the layers in order but will leave out all the layering and molding steps. You just assemble into the mold the ingredients for each layer and when you finish layering you simply press down to firm all the layers together before removing the mold then finish by wrapping and sealing the nori to create your bricks. You could also slice long bricks into halves or thirds, then serve as sandwiches rather than multiple, bite-size pieces. Or wrap each sandwich brick with cling wrap and put into lunches or save in the refrigerator for a ready to go snack. While most enjoy them at room temperature, once refrigerated, I sometimes like to warm them slightly by popping them into the microwave for about 10 – 15 seconds, covered by a moist paper towel and then allowed to cool a minute before diving into a bite.

Once you get the basic idea, move on to the recipes and

suggestions for creating what I call my *Mainland Musubi Madness.* If you watched the YouTube videos I suggested you will have already seen that there are many ways to create new sauces and ingredients to make your musubi masterpieces.

One of the easiest ways to add variety to your musubi is by changing up the sauces that you use to marinade and fry your SPAM. They will infuse your SPAM with unique flavors to suit any pallet. And then of course my suggestions for ingredients will continue to provide limitless combination ideas and inspire you to try your own layering styles.

Afterwards you may enjoy seeing the suggestions for Appetizers which includes "Musubi Rice Balls" and "Musubi Canapes" which are simply a spin on my Musubi creations, but in bite size versions that mimic the classic cracker appetizers we are all so familiar with as part of any pre-meal appetite teaser or cocktail party fare.

Lastly I give you some suggestions for putting together your own Musubi Party to prepare musubis with friends and family - this can be especially fun with the kids. Instead of a cookie baking party, why not make your next family tradition Musubi Making?!

So please enjoy the rest of this book and LET THE MUSUBI MADNESS BEGIN!

CLASSIC MUSUBI RECIPE #2
MUSUBI with Scrambled Egg

Nori
Rice
Furikake
SPAM
Scrambled EGG
Furikake
Rice

Press layers together, wrap nori tightly to make bricks. Slice brick into sandwich or appetizer size bites.

CLASSIC MUSUBI RECIPE #3
MUSUBI Katsui - Deep Fried Musubi

Nori
Rice
SPAM
Flour
Egg
Panko Crumbs
¼ cup cooking oil

Make your classic Musubi, now roll the brick in flour, dip it into an egg wash, and roll in Panko Crumbs - then deep fry a few minutes, turn and fry a few more minutes. Place on a paper towel to absorb excess oil. Slice into sushi roll pieces. Serve with dipping sauce(s).

III. MAINLAND MUSUBI MADNESS –
MUSUBI WITH A TWIST

Recipe #1 - MUSUBI CALIFORNIA ROLL

Nori
Rice
Sliced Cucumbers
SPAM
Fresh Basil (opt.)
Cream Cheese
Avocado
Rice
Press together, remove mold.
Wrap nori to form Musubi brick and slice.

Recipe #2 - MUSUBI TACO

Nori
Rice
Doritos – whole/broken – not crushed
Pico de Gallo or Salsa
Sliced or Shredded Cheddar Cheese
SPAM - sautéed and grilled in Chipotle Chili Sauce or Lowery's Taco Sauce
Drizzle of Sriracha Sauce or Red Pepper Flakes (opt.)
Iceberg Lettuce
Rice
Press together, remove mold.
Wrap nori to form Musubi brick and slice

Recipe #3 - MAC & CHEESE MUSUBI

Nori
Rice
Mac & Cheese (your favorite homemade recipe, or from a box, or from KFC)
Rice
Press together, remove mold.
Wrap nori to form Musubi brick and slice.

Tip: Using leftover Mac & Cheese that you refry is a great way to prepare

Recipe #4 - BREAKFAST MUSUBI #1

Nori
Rice
Scrambled Egg
Bacon bits or strip
SPAM spears – (opt. grilled with bacon grease)
Hash browns or tatter tots
Rice
Press together, remove mold.
Wrap nori to form Musubi brick and slice.

Recipe #5 - BREAKFAST MUSUBI #2

Pancake cut in half (instead of Nori)
Rice
Scrambled Egg
SPAM (slices or cut into spears)
Maple Syrup
Rice
Half slice of pancake
Press together, remove from mold.
Wrap with a strip of bacon around the center.

Recipe #6 - BBQ MUSUBI

Nori
Rice
Swiss cheese (or American cheese slice)
Caramelized Onions
SPAM – grilled/sautéed in BBQ, A-1 or Worcestershire sauce
Mushrooms - sautéed in butter, or Baked Beans
Rice
Press together, remove mold.
Wrap nori to form Musubi brick and slice.

Recipe #7 - OCTOBER FEST MUSUBI

Nori
Rice
Sauerkraut or Pickled Cabbage
SPAM - sautéed in a dark beer
Mustard
Rice
Press together, remove mold.
Wrap nori to form Musubi brick and slice.

Recipe #8 - TEX-MEX CHILI MUSUBI

Nori
Rice
Chili (with or w/out beans) - Or substitute Chili with Sweet Roasted Red Bell Peppers or have both!
SPAM – grilled/sautéed in Worcestershire, BBQ, or A-1
Rice
Press together, remove mold.
Wrap nori to form Musubi brick and slice.

Recipe #9 - FRUITY MUSUBI

Nori
Rice
SPAM - sautéed in any favorite jam and soy sauce
Pineapple, Mango, Banana – sliced or mashed
Fresh Mint (opt.)
Rice
Press together, remove mold.
Wrap nori to form Musubi brick and slice.

Tip: Sometimes with juicy ingredients like fruit or jelly it can be best to go lightly, or add to pan when grilling the SPAM for just the last few minutes, or try mixing with the rice first so they don't over flow – and press less firmly in mold.

Recipe #10 - SPAM & CHEESE MUSUBI

Nori
Rice
Cheddar Cheese
SPAM
Mustard and Mayonnaise (might try mixing with rice first)
Rice
Press together, remove mold.
Wrap nori to form Musubi brick and slice.

Recipe #11 – FRENCH DIP MUSUBI

Nori
Rice
Crushed Croutons - or could also bread & deep fry the musubi after assembled
SPAM - grilled and sautéed in a French Dip au juis
Mushrooms & Onions - sautéed in Au Juis (Opt.)
Rice
Press together, remove mold.
Wrap nori to form Musubi brick and slice.

Recipe #12 - CHICKEN FRIED STEAK MUSUBI

Nori
Rice
Mash Potato (or cooked red potatoes –sliced, or French fries)
Gravy
SPAM - battered and deep fried
Rice
Press together, remove mold.
Wrap nori to form Musubi brick and slice.

Recipe #13 – MUSUBI PIZZA

Nori
Rice
Mozzarella Cheese
Fresh Basil
Any of your favorite pizza toppings: onions, mushrooms, olives, bell pepper, (raw or sautéed first) and pepperoni (opt.)
Spam - grilled and sautéed in Pizza Sauce & garlic powder
Rice
Press together, remove mold.
Wrap nori to form Musubi brick and slice.

Recipe #14 – PB&J MUSUBI

Nori
Rice
Spam (opt.) – or substitute with sliced banana
Peanut Butter
Jelly
Rice
Press together, remove mold.
Wrap nori to form Musubi brick and slice.
Tip: I like to pre-mix the Peanut Butter & Jelly together before layering but could also mix with rice.

Recipe #15 – CUCUMBER & HUMUS MUSUBI

Nori
Rice
Sliced Cucumbers
Humus
Fresh Basil
SPAM
Spinach
Rice
Press together, remove mold.
Wrap nori to form Musubi brick and slice.

Recipe #16 – BLT MUSUBI

Nori
Rice
Bacon
Lettuce
SPAM – grilled and sautéed in bacon grease or butter
Pickle
Tomato (sliced)
Rice
Press together, remove mold.
Wrap nori to form Musubi brick and slice.

Recipe #17 – VEGGIE MUSUBI (anything goes)

Nori
Rice
Lettuce
Fresh Basil
Carrots (spears or julienned)
Dressing (your favorite)
Radish or Pickled Beets
Rice
Press together, remove mold.
Wrap nori to form Musubi brick and slice.

Recipe #18 - MUSUBI LEFTOVERS

Nori
Rice
Leftover Curry Noodles, Pad Thai, Lo Mein, etc.
SPAM - sautéed and grilled in Teriyaki Sauce
Rice
Press together, remove mold.
Wrap nori to form Musubi brick and slice

Recipe #19 – STIR-FRY MUSUBI

Nori
Rice
Scramble egg
Furikake Flakes
Stir Fry Veggies – sliced onion, Pre-mixed coleslaw cabbage mix fried with soy & oyster or fish sauces, sesame oil
SPAM - sautéed and grilled in Teriyaki Sauce
Rice
Press together, remove mold.
Wrap nori to form Musubi brick and slice

Recipe #20 – YOUR OWN MUSUBI CREATION

Anything your taste buds desire… for example, a friend of mine who tried the French Dip Musubi has already suggested adding grilled asparagus spears…so let your imagination run wild!

IV. APPETIZERS & TINY TASTE TREATS - Quick and Simple

MUSUBI RICE BALLS

Basically this appetizer is just what it sounds like, a ball of rice with various toppings. While I have heard rice balls are traditionally only served at funerals, I don't believe we on the Mainland should limit them to only somber occasions.

To make these quick and easy appetizers all you do is take a spoonful of sushi rice and plop it onto a sheet of cling wrap. Next, you gather up the cling wrap around the rice and twist and twist until it forms a tight ball. Then, simply remove the cling wrap and set on a cookie sheet. Make as many rice balls as you need before starting to garnish with your toppings. You can make all the toppings the same or you can make an assortment depending on how many ingredients you want to assemble. Also, an ice cream scoop or melon baller is a handy way to start a ball shape when scooping up the rice. Remember to dip in water first to prevent rice sticking. You can also add Furikake flakes to the rice before squeezing into a ball or, roll the rice ball in Furikake flakes to completely coat the outside.

Now you begin adding your toppings: - Just some of the varieties you can try:

*Rice Ball with a square of cheddar or other favorite cheese on top, then add SPAM and topped with smelt eggs and a little green onion. – *Tip:* For a decorative look, you can use mini cookie cutters to cut out shapes of cheese and SPAM.

Other suggestions for Rice Ball Appetizers:

*Try this same version but substitute scrambled egg for the cheese.

*Rice Ball with thin slice of cucumber and a small chunk of cream cheese and topped with a dollop of sriracha-mayonase.

*Rice Ball with SPAM, cucumber topped with sweet roasted red bell pepper.

*Rice Ball with SPAM, cucumber topped with sauerkraut and dollop of sour cream.

* Rolled in flour, egg wash and panko crumbs then deep fried.

The combinations are endless so use your imagination. You might even try taking a chunk of cream cheese and wedges of cucumber and SPAM and then wrapping the rice ball around them to create a "stuffed rice ball."

Another trick for rice balls would be to grill SPAM in your favorite sauce, teriyaki, pineapple etc., then chop up the spam in a food processer or slice and chop with a knife. Next mix chopped SPAM with rice and Furikake seasoning and roll into a ball as usual. You could stack this on top of a square of cheddar or Swiss cheese and a little chunk of pineapple on top and skewered with a long toothpick.

. You can also buy mini molds and wrap narrow pre-cut strips of nori around them for Musubi "Poppers!"

MUSUBI CANAPES

Again, just like they sound, little open faced appetizers, but instead of crackers you make little squares of rice layered on top or with layers of Nori and any other combination of ingredients to create bite size snacks. You can create these free formed however, the press is especially nice to give you uniformed bricks to pile your ingredients onto.

So start with a sheet of nori, place mold on top and fill with a layer of rice. Now you can press this first layer down and remove the mold, or you can add another layer of anything you like before adding one more layer of rice, pressing down and removing the mold. Then slice into individual bite-size squares or rectangles before you add topping in layers of cheese, olives, glazed onions, Furikake, cucumbers, water chestnuts, pickles, cream cheese, sriracha-mayonase or even fruit and sour cream. Just let your imagination and pallet guide you to creations that mix sweet with sour or savory groupings. Add dressing and sauces in drizzles or dots. Try building what would be a typical cracker or veggie type appetizer with the addition of the rice and SPAM for a unique flavor and texture.

V. GLOSSARY OF INGREDIENTS

SAUCES – Ready made or mix your own

Teriyaki
BBQ
Fruit - Cherry, Berry, Pineapple, Mango, Marmalade, Banana, Apple
Granulated Sugar
Brown Sugar
Molasses or Maple Syrup

Worcestershire Sauce
Orange Juice
Cranberry Juice
Sour Cream
French Dip
Ginger
Soy sauce
Sesame Seed Oil

SPREADS -

Cream Cheese
Dressings: Ranch, Blue Cheese, French, Italian
Jams and Jellies
Ketchup, Mustard, Mayo, Relish
Peanut Butter
Sour Cream

Sriracha
Sriracha-Mayonnaise
Thai Peanut Sauce
Anything else you like…

IGREDIENTS - All the goodies that go inside!

- **RICE** – steamed white sushi rice, or why not use steamed brown rice if you prefer.

- **SPAM** - grilled and sautéed to flavor; battered and deep fried; or purchase any one of the numerous - flavored SPAM varieties.

* And any one or more of these:

Apple
Avocado
Bacon
Banana
Basil
Bell Pepper
Bean Sprouts
Beans, black or chili
Cabbage - green or red, cooked, raw or pickled
Carrot
Celery
Cheddar Cheese - or assorted deli cheeses
Chicken
Chili con Carne
Chips – potato, BBQ, your favorite
Coleslaw
Crackers – pick your favorite
Cream Cheese
Croutons
Cucumber
Doritos
Egg – scramble, fried, hard boiled
French Fries
Furikake Rice Seasonings
Garlic Powder
Ginger
Goldfish Crackers (Hash Browns)
Hatches Green Chili
Honey
Humus
Imitation Crabmeat
Jalapeños
Jams & Jellies
Kimchi
Lettuce – iceberg, red leaf, romaine
Mac & Cheese
Mango

Mint
Noodles
Olives - black or green
Onion – raw, white, red, caramelized
Onion Rings
Pancake
Peanuts and other crushed nuts
Peanut Butter
Pico de Gallo
Pineapple
Potato - fries, mashed, tater tots
Pretzels

Red Pepper Flakes
Roasted Red Bell Peppers
Roasted Sesame Seeds
Salsa
Saluted Mushrooms
Sauerkraut
Shrimp
Spinach
Steak
Sweet Potato
Tofu
Tomato
Tuna
Wasabi
Zucchini

Keep Going - Anything else you can possibly think of to try! You are only limited by your own imagination and tastes.

Tip: Goldfish, chips and crackers – depending on what you use, you may want to crush or place on top of a layer that will act as a binder such as mayo, chili, salsa, etc. to hold in place.

****

VI. MUSUBI MAKING PARTY

So now that you know how to Musubi - and how to "mix it up," why not get your family and friends together for a **Musubi Making Party**? Introduce your new found talent and see what everyone comes up with as you lay out an assortment of ingredients, a la Musubi Bar, just as you would put together your own taco, hot dog, or burger fixings. You can make it as simple or as challenging as you like. Use a limited number of ingredients or prepare a greater selection to choose from and see what you get.

OCCASIONS TO MAKE MUSUBI
When and Where to Musubi:

- **Make them as a gift** for someone that you know has tried and loves musubis.

- **Make ahead of time and pack** for your next road trip, vacation, golf outing or other sports event.

- **Make them as an after game snack** for the soccer or football or little league team or gymnastics meet.

- **Why not make musubis for a fund raiser instead of a bake sale?** Here I recommend creating a simple favorite or two and perhaps making some samples either in the form of mini-musubi or the musubi balls and canapés using the same ingredients as your full size musubi offerings.

➢ **Make them for parties, showers, brunch, and holidays** – great for celebrations.

➢ **Anytime, anywhere, any occasion**…

VII. FINAL THOUGHTS

Thank you for purchasing this book and giving me the opportunity to share with you my love of this delicious sandwich and sushi-like snack. I hope that after reading it and checking out the tutorials on YouTube, or perusing the Pins at Pinterest - which all show a great variety of musubi inspiration by others who make musubi - that you will try these tasty treats and find them very much to your liking. And even if you never wish to make some of the variations described, I hope that you will at least attempt to make some of the classic recipes to enjoy again and again for lunch or to take to your next gathering and continue to spread the word to the masses that the Marvelous Musubi may become a standard treat for any occasion. And please check out my website and post comments or share your musubi stories: http://moshimoshiworld.wordpress.com

Lastly, I would like to say a special thanks to my family and friends who have supported me in all my creative efforts no matter how crazy they might seem. Wishing you many Oyshee moments! Enjoy!

****

About the Author:

Debra D. Hayashi is a Colorado author who enjoys living in the Denver area while she writes children's books, designs and creates jewelry and mixed media art. She is also a singer songwriter. This is her first Cookbook. Her Children's books include: *It's A Puppy Dog Christmas* – a Read along/Sing along Christmas tale available as a hardcover book and as an audio e-book at http://www.blurb.com/b/4681861-it-s-a-puppy-dog-christmas-by-debra-d-hayashi Her second book: *Bogey Beagle and his Totally Terrific Storm Tamer Shirt* is the story of a dog and how he handles a special problem with the help of his friend Ellie. Find it at Amazon.com http://www.amazon.com/s/ref=nb_sb_noss?url=search-alias%3Daps&field-keywords=bogey+beagle
Debra is currently working on another Children's Story – *Little Yakamashii* – a "Modern" Classic Fairy Tale about a little girl with a very loud voice. When she is not writing, designing and creating, Debra enjoys spending time with her husband, and their two Samoyed dogs, Keiko and Trio.

Look for her on Twitter at https://twitter.com/ddhayashi1?ref_src=twsrc%5Etfw, her blogs https://moshimoshiworld.wordpress.com/ at and https://bogeybeagle.com/

Made in the USA
Las Vegas, NV
02 March 2025